W9-DFT-227

BE AN
ACTIVE CITIZEN
AT YOUR SCHOOL

Helen Mason

🌲 Crabtree Publishing Company
www.crabtreebooks.com

CITIZENSHIP IN ACTION

Author: Helen Mason

Series research and development: Reagan Miller

Editors: Petrice Custance and Reagan Miller

Proofreader: Janine Deschenes

Design and photo research: Margaret Amy Salter

Prepress technician: Margaret Amy Salter

Print and production coordinator: Katherine Berti

Photographs

Ammit Jack / Shutterstock.com
All other images from Shutterstock

Library and Archives Canada Cataloguing in Publication

Mason, Helen, 1950-, author
    Be an active citizen at your school / Helen Mason.

(Citizenship in action)
Includes index.
Issued in print and electronic formats.
ISBN 978-0-7787-2600-5 (hardback).--
ISBN 978-0-7787-2606-7 (paperback).--ISBN 978-1-4271-1777-9 (html)

    1. Citizenship--Study and teaching--Juvenile literature. 2. Democracy--
Study and teaching--Juvenile literature. 3. Civics--Study and teaching--Juvenile
literature. 4. Social participation--Juvenile literature. 5. Political participation--
Juvenile literature. I. Title.

LC1091.M38 2016   j370.11'5   C2016-904146-8
                                        C2016-904147-6

Library of Congress Cataloging-in-Publication Data

CIP available at the Library of Congress

8083

Crabtree Publishing Company

www.crabtreebooks.com   1-800-387-7650

Printed in Canada/082016/TL20160715

Published in Canada
Crabtree Publishing
616 Welland Ave.
St. Catharines, Ontario
L2M 5V6

Published in the United States
Crabtree Publishing
PMB 59051
350 Fifth Avenue, 59th Floor
New York, New York 10118

Published in the United Kingdom
Crabtree Publishing
Maritime House
Basin Road North, Hove
BN41 1WR

Published in Australia
Crabtree Publishing
3 Charles Street
Coburg North
VIC 3058

What is in this book?

What is a community?

A **community** is a place where people live, work, and play. Your home is a small community. Your city or town is a large community. Your country is also a community.

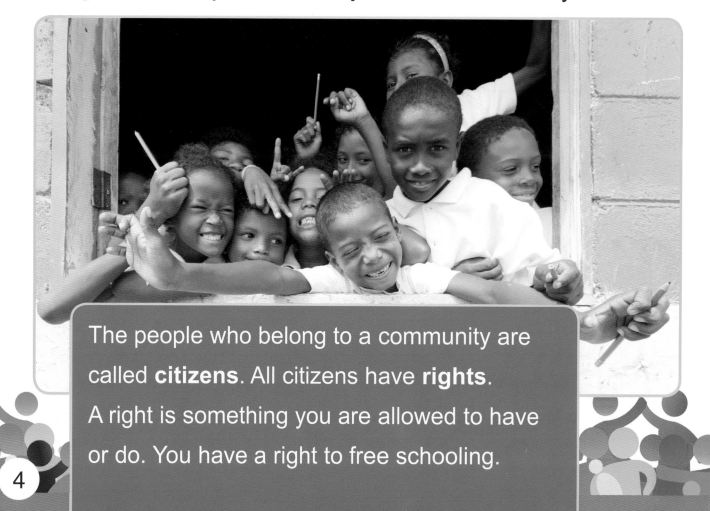

The people who belong to a community are called **citizens**. All citizens have **rights**. A right is something you are allowed to have or do. You have a right to free schooling.

Citizens also have a **responsibility** to make their community a great place for everyone. A responsibility is something you should take care of or do. You have a responsibility to cooperate with your teachers.

You have a right to play in public parks.

My school community

Everyone who works at your school is part of its community. You are a member of the school community. So are the teachers, the principal, custodians, bus drivers, and volunteers.

All of these people work together to make the school a safe and fun place to learn.

As a member of the community, you have rights and responsibilities. You have a right to take books out of the library. You have a responsibility to take care of and return those books.

You have a right to use the gym. You are responsible for wearing gym shoes.

What is an active citizen?

Active citizens work hard to make their school community a fun and safe place. Active citizens follow these rules:

1. **They show respect.** This means to be courteous. Active citizens speak politely to other students, teachers, and staff.

2. **They play fair.** This includes following game and school rules. It also means giving others a chance to speak and share.

3. They act responsibly. Active citizens come to school with the things they need, such as completed homework and gym shoes.

These rules make school fun for everyone!

What do you think?

Which images on this page show active citizens helping their community? Which images do not show active citizens?

What is a class meeting?

Every day, Ava's class starts with a class meeting. They talk about ways to make their school community a great place for everyone.

- ✓ Everyone sits in a circle.
- ✓ They talk about a problem they want to solve.
- ✓ Everyone has a turn to speak.
- ✓ They explain how they feel about the problem.
- ✓ They listen to each other.

Today, they are talking about
all the garbage on the floor after lunch.

"How can we work together to solve this
problem?" the teacher asks.

"Get a second garbage can," Mason says.

"Recycle the wrapping," suggests Mia.

"Go home for lunch," Alex says.

"Take your garbage home," Anna suggests.

What do you think?

What is your suggestion to solve this problem?

Building consensus

Ava's class continues to discuss the garbage problem. The students ask each other questions to better understand each other's ideas.

"Can we pack lunches that do not make any garbage?" Austin asks.

"I can help," Ameena says. "My mother has many containers we can use to pack up our lunches."

"I like pears," Max says. "Can I throw out the core?"

"We could **compost** it instead" Gil says.

Juan listens to the ideas and writes them down. The students have decided on three ways to best meet their goal. They have reached **consensus**.

Our Litterless Lunch Plan

Our class agrees to:

 Bring food in reusable containers. Take them home.

 Use a thermos or plastic container for drinks.

 Compost food that is left over.

Everyone in the class listened, shared ideas, and worked together to create a plan.

Voting

Mr. Gavin's Grade Two class would like to do something special for their school community. They **brainstorm** ideas for a full week.

Three ideas have a lot of support. Lily writes them on the board.

sports equipment

library books

picnic tables

The class decides to **vote**.
Each student has one vote.

Jayden hands each student a **ballot**.
They put an X beside their choice.

The ballots are collected and counted.
The choice of library books has
received the most votes.

There are many ways to vote. This student votes by raising his hand.

Planning an event

The students must raise money to buy the library books for their school. They decide to hold a dance-a-thon. They plan the event.

Who? Students in Mr. Gavin's class

What? They will dance the chicken dance for 30 minutes. They will ask people to donate money for each minute of dancing.

When? The first Friday of March

Where? In the school library

How? Jack will bring the music. Emma will teach the dance. Grade 2s will practice before the event.

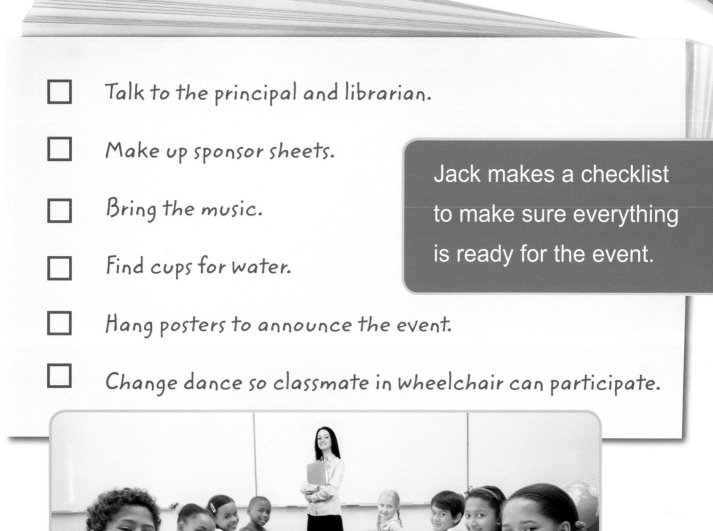

☐ Talk to the principal and librarian.

☐ Make up sponsor sheets.

☐ Bring the music.

☐ Find cups for water.

☐ Hang posters to announce the event.

☐ Change dance so classmate in wheelchair can participate.

Jack makes a checklist to make sure everything is ready for the event.

Solving problems together

Other classes want to be active citizens and help with the school dance-a-thon. Gina reports this at a class meeting. The students talk about a change of plan.

Who? The whole school.

What? They will dance the chicken dance for 30 minutes. They will ask people to donate money for each minute of dancing.

When? The first Friday of March.

Where? In the school gym.

How? They will run the music over the school sound system. Grade 2s will teach the dance to all other grades during gym class.

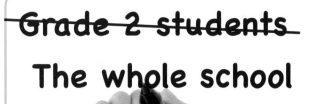

~~Grade 2 students~~
The whole school

The class makes changes until they reach a consensus. Everyone is happy with the new plan.

In the ~~library~~ school gym

Caring and sharing

The dance-a-thon brings in a lot of money. The students are very proud! They choose 100 books for their library. There is still money left. The students brainstorm ways to spend the extra money. David writes down the ideas.

- ☐ Buy baseball bats, balls, and helmets.
- ☐ Start a school breakfast program.
- ☐ Choose plants for the school garden.
- ☐ Buy and plant trees.
- ☐ Donate to a charity.
- ☐ Help refugees who are new to our community.
- ☐ Buy clothes for homeless people.
- ☐ Sponsor a child in another country.

What do you think?

How would you spend the extra money? How could you be an active citizen to help your school?

Dear sponsor,
Thank you!

Love,
Amara

Learning more

Books

Kopp, Megan. *Be the Change for the Environment*.
Crabtree Publishing Company, 2015.

Murphy, Stuart J. *Earth Day—Hooray!* HarperCollins, 2004.

Welbourn, Shannon. *Be the Change in your School.*
Crabtree Publishing Company, 2015.

Web Sites

Help improve the air quality at your school by starting a no idling program:
http://captainplanetfoundation.org/planeteers/youth-planeteer-clubs/wind/

Learn about bullying and how to stop it:
http://pbskids.org/itsmylife/friends/bullies/

Watch a video on being a good citizen at school:
www.hrmvideo.com/catalog/school-rules-being-a-good-citizen-at-school

Words to know

ballot (BAL-it) noun A piece of paper used in voting

brainstorm (BRANE-storm) verb List all ideas to help make a decision

citizens (CIT-i-zens) noun People who belong to a community

community (CU-mu-ni-tee) noun A place where people live, work, and play

consensus (cun-SEN-sus) noun When everyone in the group agrees

compost (KOM-pos) verb To mix fruit and vegetable waste and allow it to rot

responsibility (re-SPONS-i-bill-i-tee) noun Something you should take care of or do

right (RITE) noun Something a person is allowed to have or do

vote (VOAT) verb Make a choice by marking a ballot or some other method, such as raising your hand

A noun is a person, place, or thing.

A verb is an action word that tells you what someone or something does.

Index

About the author

When Helen Mason was in grade 1, she sold donuts to raise money for a school fundraiser. She continues to volunteer at community events, including school fun fairs. This is her 32nd book.